The Abilities We Have

Alyssa Weaver
Illustrated by i Cenizal

The Abilities We Have
Copyright © 2022 by Alyssa Weaver

All rights reserved. No part of this publication may be reproduced, distributed, or transmitted in any form or by any means, including photocopying, recording, or other electronic or mechanical methods, without the prior written permission of the author, except in the case of brief quotations embodied in critical reviews and certain other non-commercial uses permitted by copyright law.

Tellwell Talent
www.tellwell.ca

ISBN
978-0-2288-4545-4 (Hardcover)
978-0-2288-4544-7 (Paperback)
978-0-2288-4546-1 (eBook)

Throughout this book you can listen and learn.
Ask questions if you wish. Do not be concerned!

Do you know what a disability is? Maybe you have a friend or a family member with a disability. Maybe you have seen a car park like this one. Maybe you have visited an all-ability playground.

Timmy is blind. He cannot see, yet he can play the piano and is never out of key.

He can read books like you and me. There is no real limit to what he can achieve!

Jason is an amputee, but he will never miss a three-pointer from behind the key.

He is a basketballer who plays in the big league – a Paralympian!
Now that's some real talent. Wouldn't you agree?

Tyler is deaf. She cannot hear, but don't be afraid if she disappears. She's a magician, you know. And she can put on a show with bunnies, a hat, and fun things like that!

We can use our hands in a way called Sign.
Hello and thank you are two favourites of mine!

Danny lives with Tourette's. She can have uncontrollable tics, but nothing compares to what comes from her lips.

She is able to sing both high notes and lows. Your jaw will drop at her spectacular shows!

Nix lives with dwarfism. He is shorter than most, but you should see what he does by the coast. He is a photographer who shoots dolphins jumping in groups!

His pictures are perfect for posters and postcards. They sell by the sea to be purchased by you and me.

Mason lives with Down syndrome. He was born with an extra chromosome, but what makes him so special is quite well known.

He's a model you may see in magazines and more. Just watch him take over the runway floor!

Sophie lives with cerebral palsy and may use her wheelchair at times. Her speech is slurred but will be heard when she collects her Nobel Prize.

She's a scientist who studies seven days a week. The experiments she conducts will surely make you screech.

A disability does not define anyone of any kind.
It is only one piece of their puzzle called life.

So now that you have met a few of my friends, just remember our book is not where it ends... Every day is a chance to learn and make new friends at every turn.

www.ingramcontent.com/pod-product-compliance
Lightning Source LLC
LaVergne TN
LVHW072114060526
838200LV00061B/4892